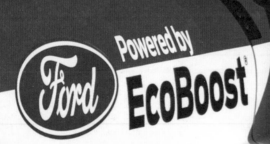

Additional images from Shutterstock.com

Louis Weber, CEO
Publications International, Ltd.
8140 Lehigh Avenue
Morton Grove, IL 60053

Permission is never granted for commercial purposes.

ISBN: 978-1-64030-274-7

Manufactured in China.

8 7 6 5 4 3 2 1

PHOTOGRAPHY:

Mirco DeCet: 44-45, 96-97, 102-103, 104-105; **Steen Fleron:** 38-39; **Mitch Frumpkin:** 78-79; **David Gooley:** 48-49, 62-63; **Sam Griffith:** 50-51; **Don Heiny:** 56-57; **Bud Juneau:** 30-31; **Milt Kieft:** 10-11; **Vince Manocchi:** 12-13, 16-17, 32-33, 34-35, 36-37, 38-39, 50-51, 52-53, 54-55, 58-59, 60-61, 64-65, 66-67, 72-73, 76-77, 94-95; **Doug Mitchel:** 18-19, 20-21, 40-41, 74-75; **David Newhardt:** 88-89; **Nina Padgett:** 26-27; **Phil Toy:** 24-25, 68-69, 80-81; **Nicky Wright:** 6-7, 14-15, 22-23, 28-29, 42-43, 46-47, 54-55, 70-71.

OWNERS:

Tom Barratt: 6-7; **Bell and Collville Motors:** 102-103; **T.W. Bernstein:** 16-17; **The Brumos Collection:** 18-19; **Cars of San Francisco:** 24-25; **Bernie Chase:** 32-33, 34-35, 36-37, 72-73; **Classic Cars of La Jolla:** 88-89; **Edward Cline:** 62-63; **Thomas R. Coady Jr:** 20-21; **Patrick and Kay Collins:** 60-61; **Allen Cummins:** 50-51; **Briggs Cunningham:** 8-9; **Richard A. Emry:** 46-47; **Alfred Ferrara:** 10-11; **Dennis Gatson:** 38-39; **Frank Gallogly:** 56-57; **Dave and Mary Glass:** 50-51; **Ellen Goodman:** 74-75; **Torben Hansen:** 38-39; **D. Heming:** 42-43; **Tim John:** 44-45; **W. Michael King:** 58-59; **John Ling:** 48-49; **Dr. L. Philip Lufty:** 28-29; **Bruce Meyer:** 52-53; **Thomas Mittler:** 22-23; **Harvey Moyes:** 66-67; **Gerald Nell:** 26-27; **Robert J. Pond Automobile Collection:** 54-55, 76-77; **Hilary Raab:** 54-55, 70-71; **James L. Roman:** 30-31; **Jeff Stephan:** 64-65; **Brooks Stevens Museum:** 14-15; **Dr. Robert Sutter:** 12-13; **Jeffrey A. and Silvia Sykes:** 68-69.

Special thanks to the following manufacturers who supplied us with additional imagery.

Aston Martin Lagonda Limited, Bugatti Automobiles S.A.S., Daimler AG, Ferrari S.p.A,, Fiat Chrysler Automobiles, Ford Motor Company, General Motors Company, Honda Motor Co., Ltd., Koenigsegg Automotive AB, Automobili Lamborghini S.p.A., McLaren Automotive, Panoz, LLC, Porsche AG, Saleen Automotive, Spyker N.V.

INDEX

P.	SUPERCAR	P.	SUPERCAR
6	1928 Mercedes-Benz SSK	76	1985 Ferrari 288 GTO
8	1933 Bugatti Type 55	78	1985 DeTomaso Pantera
10	1936 Duesenberg SSJ	80	1987 Ferrari Testarossa
12	1936 Jaguar SS-100	82	1988 Ferrari F40
14	1938 Talbot-Lago	84	1988 Porsche 959
16	1952-54 Allard J2X	86	1989 Lamborghini Countach
18	1952 Maserati A6G	88	1990 Chevrolet Corvette ZR1
20	1953 Cunningham C-3	90	1990 Lamborghini Diablo
22	1953 Ferrari 342 America	92	1991 Vector W-8
24	1956 Mercedes-Benz 300SL Gullwing	94	1992 Dodge Viper
26	1957 Chevrolet Corvette Fuel Injection	96	1992 Jaguar XJ220
28	1957 Jaguar XK-SS	98	1994 Aston Martin DB7
30	1959 BMW 507	100	1996 Dodge Viper
32	1961 Ferrari 250 GT SWB Berlinetta	102	1996 Lotus Esprit
34	1962 Ferrari 250 GT Spyder California	104	1996 McLaren F1
36	1962 Ferrari 250 GTO	106	2000 Panoz Esperante
38	1963 Jaguar E-Type roadster	108	2001 Chevrolet Corvette Z06
40	1964 Porsche 904 GTS	110	2002 Lamborghini Murcielago
42	1965 Sunbeam Tiger	112	2003 Dodge Viper
44	1965 TVR Griffith	114	2003 Ferrari Enzo
46	1966 Shelby GT-350	116	2003 Saleen S7
48	1967 Bizzarrini GT Strada 5300	118	2004 Porsche Carrera GT
50	1967 Chevrolet Corvette 427	120	2005 Bugatti Veyron
52	1967 Shelby Cobra 427 SC	122	2005 Ford GT
54	1968 Ferrari 356 GTB/4 Daytona	124	2005 Mercedes-Benz SLR
56	1968 Ford GT40	126	2015 Chevrolet Corvette Z06
58	1969 DeTomaso Mangusta	128	2016 Lamborghini Aventador S
60	1970 Chevrolet Corvette roadster LS5	130	2017 Acura NSX
62	1971 Jaguar Series III E-Type V-12 Roadster	132	2017 Bugatti Chiron
64	1972 Lamborghini Miura SV	134	2017 Ferrari LaFerrari
66	1973 Maserati Bora	136	2017 Ford GT
68	1973 Porsche 911 Carrera RS	138	2018 Dodge Demon
70	1975 Ferrari 365 GTB BB	140	2018 Koenigsegg Agere RS
72	1975 Lamborghini LP400 Countach	142	2018 McLaren 720S
74	1980 BMW M1	144	2018 Spyker C8 Preliator

MERCEDES-BENZ
Model SSK 1928

Mercedes-Benz built winning race cars and sporty touring models in the early 1900s, but its first true roadgoing sports car was the Model S of 1927. Relatively large and heavy in the German manner, the S packed a supercharged six-cylinder engine designed by the talented Ferdinand Porsche. The SSK was a lighter, more powerful version. Horsepower was 170 normal, 225 with the "blower" engaged, enough to make this one of the world's fastest cars at the time with a top speed of around 120 mph. A lighter SSKL model followed with even higher performance. Many SSK chassis got custom coachwork, such as this cabriolet with a Corsica body. Note the exhaust pipes exiting the hood.

Italian Ettore Bugatti settled in France to build *pur sang* (pure-blood) cars starting in 1910. Bugattis were models of meticulous, weight-efficient engineering, as his roadgoing sports cars were often based on his winning race-car designs. Among Bugatti's best road cars was the Type 55, a dashing roadster designed by Ettore's talented son Jean. Its chassis was lifted from Bugatti's contempoary Type 51 single-seat racing car, as was the supercharged 2.3-liter twincam straight-eight, detuned to 135 bhp but capable of up to 112 mph. Only 38 T55s were built between 1932 and 1935.

BUGATTI
Type 55 1933

DUESENBERG
SSJ 1936

After achieving fame for their winning race-car engines, brothers Fred and August Duesenberg teamed with tycoon E.L. Cord to create "the world's finest motorcar." Bowing in late 1928, the Duesenberg Model J was big, heavy, opulent, and ultra costly, but also America's fastest, most technically advanced car. A supercharged SJ soon followed with at least 320 bhp and up to 140 mph flat-out. Shown here is one of two short-chassis SSJ roadsters with the engine tuned to produce 400 bhp. It was as close to a sports car as a Deusey ever got.

JAGUAR
SS-100 1936

The first sports car named Jaguar appeared in 1936 from William Lyons' SS Cars, Ltd., an outgrowth of Swallow Sidecars, the motorcycle-sidecar business he started in the 1920s. A follow-up to the previous year's SS90, the SS-Jaguar 100 came with either a 2.7-liter straight-six or a new, more potent 3.5-liter unit. The latter could deliver 0-60 mph in under 11 seconds and over 100 mph flat out, sensational for a non-supercharged car in those days. Handling and roadholding were first rate, too. The styling—classically correct but sleek and slow slung—was largely Lyons' own work. Alas, only 314 of these cars could be built before war came to Britain in 1939.

TALBOT-LAGO
1938

In 1935, Major Anthony Lago took the helm at the old-line Sunbeam-Talbot-Darracq company. He immediately staked its future on high-performance cars that could double as competitive racers. Though not that successful on the track, Talbot-Lagos were wonderful on the road, thanks to a new 140-bhp 4.0-liter straight-six and a well-sorted chassis. This is one of a handful of "teardrop" coupes bodied by Figoni et Falaschi. Original price was $17,500, a towering sum for the day.

ALLARD
J2X 1952-54

Sydney Allard built crude but fast cars such as the 1950–51 J2 and, pictured here, the J2X of 1952–54. Both were designed as racing cars that could be used on the road if need be. The X boasted an improved front suspension requiring an extended frame, hence the suffix letter, plus an outside, instead of concealed, spare tire. Allard still favored Ford/Mercury flathead V8s, but also listed potent new overhead-valve engines from Cadillac and Chrysler. Suitably powered, these English Allards were popular low-buck rides for period American road racers and were always a threat, though difficult to drive. But rivals soon surpassed the low-tech J2 and J2X, so Allard gave up after turning out just 90 and 83, respectively.

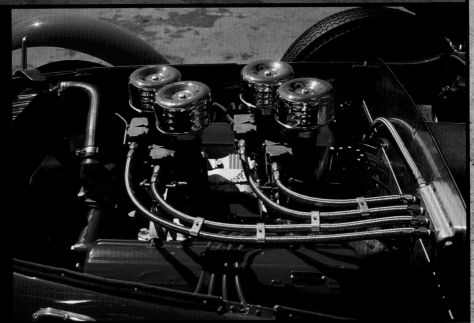

MASERATI
A6G 1952

Maserati issued a more ambitious roadgoing sports car in 1951, the A6G, available with a variety of coachbuilt coupe and convertible bodies. A new 2.0-liter overhead-cam inline six sat in the basic chassis of the superseded A6/1500 series but delivered 100 bhp instead of 65. But that was no match for Ferrari in European formula racing, so Maserati substituted a twincam version with 150 horsepower for revised 1954 models dubbed A6G/2000. This engine was originally developed for racing, debuting in 1947. The cars it first powered, designated A6GS, were trim single-seat affairs with cycle-wing fenders. A two-seat "flared wing" version was also developed for sports-car contests, with body design by Gugliemo Carraoli. Completed in 1952, it was basically a prototype and the only one of its kind. It survives today as shown here. An improved "Series II" A6GS with modern slab-sided styling appeared in 1954.

Briggs Cunningham devised the touring C-3 mainly to qualify his race cars as "production"—and fend off scrutiny from the IRS. Only 27 were built in 1953–55: nine convertibles and 18 coupes. All used the basic C-2R chassis, Chrysler hemi V8, and handsome, well-appointed Vignale bodies designed by Giovanni Michelotti. Despite eye-popping $9000-$10,000 prices, demand for the C-3 exceeded Briggs' ability to supply.

CUNNINGHAM
C-3 1953

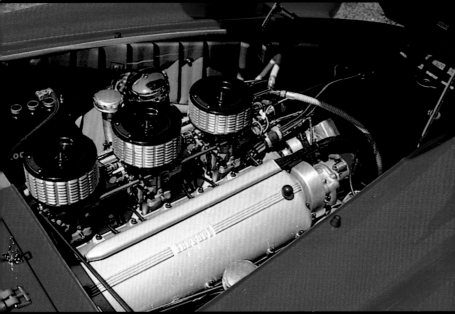

In 1950, engineer Aurelio Lampredi designed a big new 4.1-liter V12 for competition Ferraris, including four named 340 Mexico after Ferrari's 1-2 win in the 1951 Mexican Road Race. Three of these cars were berlinettas like this Vignale-bodied exercise; the fourth was a roadster. The Lampredi V12 was detuned for road use in 1952, when it was coupled with a revised chassis for Ferrari's first "deluxe" touring cars, named 342 America. The following year brought a replacement 375 America with power boosted from 200 to 300. All these early Ferraris are highly prized rarites.

One of the most recognized and coveted of sports cars, the Mercedes-Benz 300SL "Gullwing" coupe was evolved from the 1952 SL prototypes that won that year's LeMans 24 Hours and marathon Mexican Road Race. U.S. import-car baron Max Hoffman convinced Daimler-Benz to offer a production model by ordering 1000 of them. As on the racers, the flip-up doors stemmed from the need to preserve rigidity in a high-sided multi-tube space-frame chassis, but they were distinctive and would be much copied in later years. The only engine was a 3.0-liter six with mechanical fuel injection. Horsepower was a stout 240, fed through a four-speed gearbox. Unveiled in early 1954, the Gullwing sold for a princely $7000-plus. That and its semi-handbuilt nature conspired to limit production to around 1400 units.

MERCEDES-BENZ
300SL GULLWING 1956

CHEVROLET
CORVETTE FUEL INJECTION 1957

Corvette had more fire for '57 with a V8 enlarged to 283 cubic inches. The five versions offered 220 to a thumping 283 horsepower, the last via "Ramjet" fuel injection, a costly $500 option. Only 240 "fuelie" '57s were built, each wearing i.d. badges on fenders and trunklid. A late-season four-speed gearbox option and stump-pulling axle ratios trimmed 0-60 mph to as little as six seconds. Total Corvette sales moved up to 6339 for the model year.

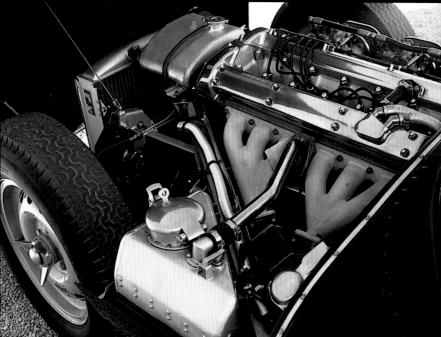

Among the raciest sports cars ever, the Jaguar XKSS was essentially a roadgoing version of the LeMans-winning D-Type, with only the barest concessions to off-track driving. Among them were a larger windshield, windshield wipers, an opening door for the passenger, and a rudimentary folding top. Yet the D-Type was surprisingly tractable and civilized on the street, so the XKSS was too. It was also about as swift, capable of 0-60 mph in under 5 seconds and a sub-14-second standing quarter-mile. Unfortunately, a mere 16 of these cars were completed when Jaguar decided to end production of both the SS and D-Type following a disastrous factory fire in February 1957. Despite its greater rarity, the XKSS went racing just like its track-bred sister, usually running in production classes, occasionally as a sports / racing prototype. Though no one knew it at the time, the XKSS forecast the general look of the future roadgoing E-Type. Also predictive was the hood/front fenders assembly that tilted up to provide fast, easy powertrain access, a boon in the heat of competition. In this scene, however, driver well-being seems the chief concern.

Bavarian Motor Works struggled to resume its auto business after World War II, offering an odd mix of high-priced sedans and inexpensive license-built microcars. Yet somehow BMW managed a sleek two-seat convertible in late 1955. Designated 507, it borrowed the basic chassis and running gear of the then-current 502 "Baroque Angel" sedan and related 503 sporty coupe, but a trimmer 97.6-inch wheelbase supported handsome styling by German-American industrial designer Albrecht Goertz. With a 3.2-liter V8 sending 150 horsepower through a four-speed gearbox, the 507 took just 8.8 seconds 0-60 mph and could do over 120 mph, impressive for the 2900-pound heft. In a sense, this was BMW's Thunderbird, but also an answer to the Mercedes 300SL—and just as costly at about $9000. Only 253 were built, mostly by hand, through 1959.

BMW
507 1959

Long regarded as one of the finest race-and-ride sports cars ever made, the Ferrari 250 GT SWB Berlinetta premiered in October 1959 to replace the longer 250 GT "Tour de France" coupe offered since 1956. Ferrari by now virtually owned the yearly race around the perimeter of France, hence the earlier car's nickname. The newcomer was even better suited to road racing, being lighter on a tighter 94.5-inch wheelbase. Ferraristi use "SWB"--short wheelbase--to distinguish it from the predecessor "TDF." The SWB introduced several internal improvements to the 250 GT-series' 3.0-liter overhead-cam Columbo V12 that added 20 horsepower for a total of 280. As usual, drive was through a four-speed manual transmission. Emphasizing the SWB's dual-purpose nature was a wide variety of available axle ratios ranging from a relatively rangy 3.44:1 to a screaming 4.57:1. Ferrari's chassis designs in the Fifties progressed much more slowly than its engines, so the SWB retained a familiar, proven suspension layout comprising coil springs and twin A-arms in front and a live rear axle located by semi-elliptic leaf springs and trailing arms. Four-wheel disc brakes, however, were new for roadgoing Ferraris, being phased in for long-wheelbase 250s earlier in 1959. Pininfarina, still Enzo's favorite coachbuilder, gave the SWB Berlinetta purposeful two-seater styling that still turns heads after almost 60 years. Doors, hood, and trunklid were rendered in aluminum, the rest of the body in steel, though a few full alloy-bodied cars were built. PF also created a new Spyder California on the SWB chassis for introduction in late 1960. Only 57 were built, versus 175 Berlinettas. Scarce though they were, the SWBs compiled a distinguished record on the track and were always thrilling on the road, with 0-60 mph available in 6.5-7.0 seconds on the way to a top speed of 140-150 mph. Factor in the timeless look and it's no wonder that these 250 GTs now command six-figure collector-market prices--and sometimes more. In the opinion of many, sports cars just don't come any better than this.

FERRARI
250 GT SWB BERLINETTA 1961

Ferrari's short-wheelbase 250 GT chassis always seemed to inspire Italy's carrozzeria. One of the best efforts was the Spyder California, new in 1960. Pininfarina, Il Commendatore's favorite coachbuilder, patterned the design on its earlier long-wheelbase SC, but trimmer proportions made it look even better. The SWB Spyder was advertised as "ready to race," but few owners did. The car was just too pretty to risk. Too rare, as well, as only 57 were built through 1963. No wonder they've become among the most sought-after— and expensive—collector Ferraris.

FERRARI
250 GT SPYDER CALIFORNIA 1962

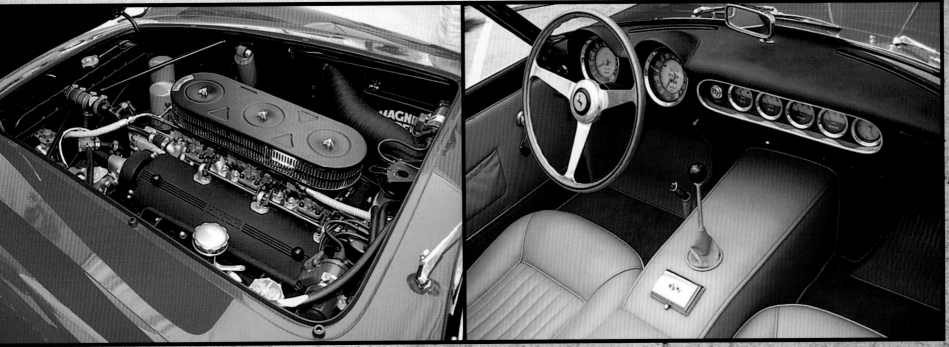

FERRARI
250 GTO 1962

A true race and ride Ferrari, the 250 GTO was announced in early '62. Though it used the same basic chassis, the GTO–"O" for homologato, approved for GT-class racing–had less weight, more power from a race-proved 3.0-liter V12, and superior aerodynamics. New U.S. world driving champ Phil Hill teamed with Olivier Gendebien to win the GT class and place second overall at both Sebring and LeMans in '62. Only 39 GTOs were built through 1964, including a few 4.0-liter and "Series II" models, plus special-body Prototype-class racers. Surprisingly docile yet very fast–5.9 seconds 0-60 mph, 0-100 in 14.1–the GTO still reigns supreme among collectible Ferraris.

A singular sensation on its 1961 Geneva, Switzerland, debut, Jaguar's slinky E-Type–called XKE in the US–picked up the general look and modified unit construction the firm had first employed for its late-1950s racing D-Type and roadgoing XKSS. Styling was again the work of Malcolm Sayer and overseen by company founder Sir William Lyons. Initially, the E-Type came with the same 3.8-liter six and all-disc brakes of the XK150, while gaining independent rear suspension. A bigger-bore 4.2-liter took over in 1964. This added 23 pound-feet of torque (to 283) but left horsepower unchanged at 265. Starting in late 1967, modifications were phased in to meet federal regulations resulting in the Series II of 1969. Larger bumper and taillights of the Series II, but with triple carburetors of the Series I, identify this convertible as a 1968 Series "1 1/2" US model, as do the "safety" rocker switches on its dashboard.

JAGUAR
E-TYPE ROADSTER 1963

The 904 GTS was conceived in 1962 as Porsche's latest GT-class endurance racer but could be used on the road given a skilled, tolerant driver. A sturdy box-rail chassis with 90.6-inch wheelbase and all-independent suspension supported a smooth fiberglass body shaped by "Butzi" Porsche, grandson of the great Ferdinand and designer of the milestone 911, which also broke cover in 1963. A five-speed 911 transaxle teamed with an engine sitting just behind the two-seater cockpit. The package was sized for the legendary 2.0-liter Carrera flat-four from the outgoing 356 series, but some 904s got six-cylinder 911 engines, and one or two were built with racing flat-eights. Though a bit heavier than planned, the 904 was fast enough and could go the distance. In 1964 alone, team entries ran 1st and 3rd in the Targa Florio, 3rd overall in the Nurburgring 1000 Kilometers, 3rd through 6th in the Tour de France, and were five of the top 12 finishers at LeMans. Only 100 were built over two years. A good many survive today and are still going strong on road and track alike.

SUNBEAM
TIGER 1965

Aimed squarely at the U.S., the Sunbeam Tiger bowed in 1964 as a beefed up Alpine with a small-block Ford V8 instead of a tame four. At around $3500, it seemed like budget Cobra. And in fact, Carroll Shelby did much of the engineering. Performance was brisk with the initial 164-horsepower 260 V8, thrilling with the 200-bhp 289 substituted for '67—as little as 7.5 seconds 0-60 mph. By that point, though, parent Rootes Group had sold out to Chrysler, which had no use for a Ford-powered car and dropped the Tiger after fewer than 7100 were built.

TVR
GRIFFITH 1965

In 1962, TVR was a small British sports-car maker not well known in the U.S. except to the likes of Jack Griffith, whose New York shops prepped racing versions of TVR's stock-in-trade model, the bobtail Grantura coupe. Just for fun, Griffith tried replacing the normal MGB four-cylinder engine with a Ford 289 V8 and found it would fit with a little work. He took the idea to cash-short TVR, which was happy to send over engineless Granturas for what Jack sold starting in 1963 as the TVR Griffith 200. Both versions wore a fiberglass body over a stout tubular backbone chassis with double-wishbone suspension and trim 85.5-inch wheelbase, but the 1905-pound Griffith packed much more power: 195 base, 271 optional. With its four-speed Ford gearbox, it could do 0-60 mph in under 6 seconds and top 150. A replacement 400 bowed in early '64 with a flat tail and better engine cooling, but events were against it and Jack gave up the following year after selling some 300 units. A few Griffiths, like this 200, were reverse-exported to Britain, complete with left-hand drive.

At Ford's behest, Carroll Shelby turned the hot-selling Mustang "ponycar" into a serious race machine, the GT-350. Modifications abounded, including a stripped-down fastback body, beefed-up chassis, and a tuned 289 V8 rated at 306 horsepower. A track-ready R-model packed at least 325 bhp. Both were high-performance bargains at $4547 and $5950, respectively. Shelby built 562 GT-350s for '65 and 2378 of the similar '66s, including 936 GT-350H models like this. The "H" stood for Hertz, which lost a bundle on weekend rentals.

BIZZARRINI
GT STRADA 5300 1967

After conjuring supercars for Ferrari and Lamborghini, maestro engineer Giotto Bizzarrini built one on his own, the GT Strada 5300. Actually, it was much like the 2+2 Iso Grifo A3L coupe he'd just designed, with a 327 Corvette V8, steel platform chassis, and a rakish Bertone-built body shaped by Giorgetto Giugiaro. But the Strada was a two-seater, had aluminum body panels instead of steel, and was built in both semi-open and fixed-roof guises. No more than 100 were built, all by hand. Each was a flyer, able to see 145 mph and run 0-60 in 6.4 seconds.

The Chevrolet Corvette Sting Ray, introduced in 1963, was the most capable 'Vette yet. The '67s were the last and cleanest Sting Rays, represented here by this lovingly restored grey ragtop with 427-cid V8. Any big-block 'Vette is now a prime collector's item. You'll pay a seven-figure price for one of the 20 cars fitted with the mighty 560-hp L88 option with special aluminum cylinder heads and lofty 12.5:1 compression ratio. Not that they often change hands. All Sting Rays featured a well organized "dual cowl" dashboard with large speedometer and tachometer and a center section containing a clock, minor controls, and radio, which mounted vertically. The 427 was introduced as the fuel-injection Corvette was phased out in 1965. Top-left is a 327-cid fuel-injected engine that developed 375 bhp.

CHEVROLET
CORVETTE 427 1967

SHELBY
COBRA 427 SC 1967

Perhaps the ultimate in raw sports-car power and performance, the legendary Shelby Cobra 427 has been widely replicated—no surprise, as only 348 originals were built in 1965–67. Though some of the copies have been quite faithful, Carroll Shelby has jealously guarded the car's name and design, even bringing lawsuits against counterfeiters. A few 427s were actually fitted with Ford's low-stress 428 passenger-car V8, whose gross horsepower is usually quoted as 355. This, however, is a genuine 427, conservatively rated at 390 bhp. Cobras have always thrilled crowds at racetracks. Though they still typically command six-figure prices as collector cars, they often compete in vintage events, evoking memories of a now-distant sports-car era.

Ferrari unveiled another instant classic in 1968 with the 365 GTB/4, which the press somehow quickly dubbed Daytona. Replacing the 275 GTB/4, it used a similar rear-transaxle chassis and an identical wheelbase but offered even higher performance thanks to a V12 enlarged from 3.3 to 4.4 liters, which took horsepower from 300 to 352. At just under $20,000, the Daytona was the costliest street Ferrari yet, but also the fastest. *Road & Track* verified the factory's claimed 174-mph top speed and timed the standing quarter-mile in just 13.8 seconds at 107.5 mph. The body design was hailed as one of Pininfarina's best, one reason for the car's long-legendary status. This berlinetta is an early European version with clear headlamp covers. U.S. models initially wore rather warty-looking exposed lights, but all later Daytonas were treated to hidden headlamps in a smooth body-color nose. The Daytona wasn't much changed otherwise, but 1969 introduced a companion spider convertible that's even more sought-after now than the coupe. Designated GTS/4, it saw only 127 copies versus nearly 1300 berlinettas. That was far too few to satisfy demand, which is why some Daytona coupes have since been decapitated to pass as spiders, an important point now for would-be owners—and judges at the ritzy car shows where these Ferraris gather.

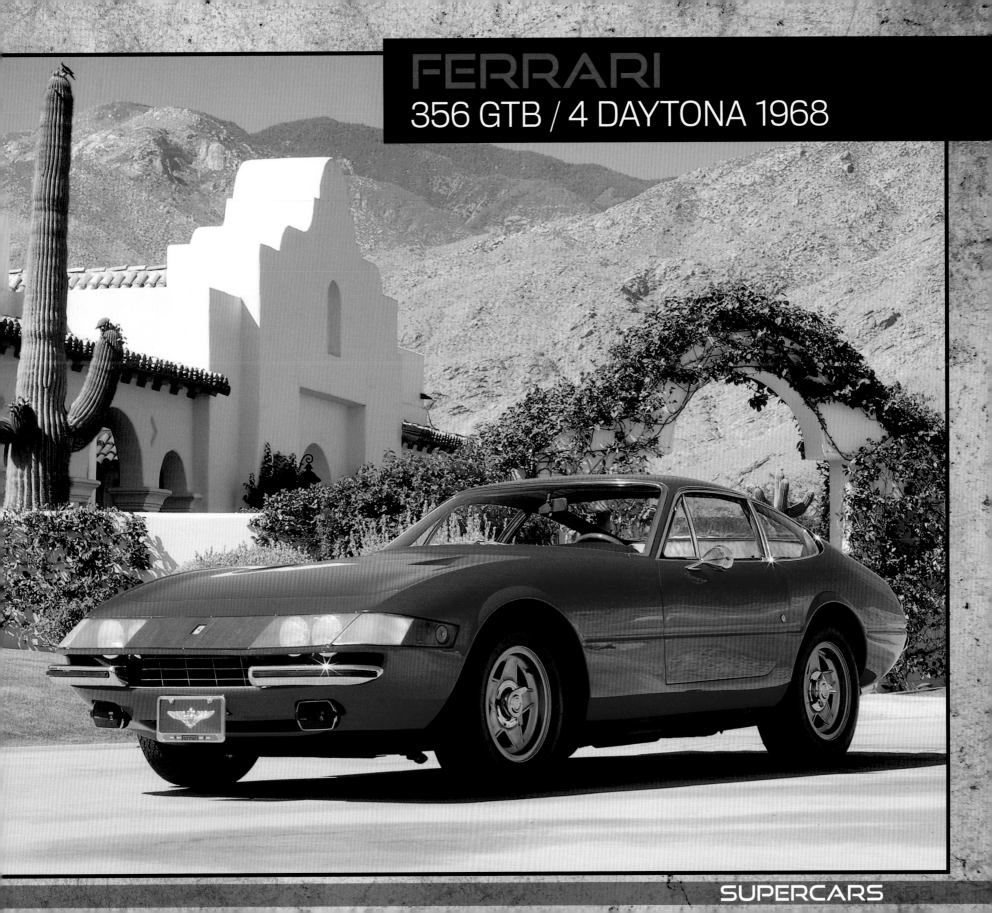

FERRARI
356 GTB / 4 DAYTONA 1968

FORD
GT40 1968

Rebuffed when it tried to buy Ferrari, Ford created the GT40 to exact revenge in international long-distance racing. The basic midengine design originated in Britain but was heavily reworked by Carroll Shelby and other Americans after a troubled 1964 debut season and scant success in '65. Ford reached the pinnacle in 1966 with smashing 1-2-3 finishes at LeMans and Daytona, thus eclipsing Ferrari at last, then repeated as world manufacturers champion and LeMans winner in 1967-69. Only 130 racing GT40s were built. Of these, 15 were Mark II versions powered by Ford big-block 427 V8s prepared by Holman & Moody of stock-car racing fame. The similar-looking Mark I used Ford's 289 small-block V8, also competition-tuned. There were also a few "Mark III" versions with long-nose bodies, detuned engines, and basic road equipment. This car is one of several Mark II replicas offered in the late 1990s by Holman & Moody scion Lee Holman. Fittingly, it was crafted with original GT40 tooling, which had somehow survived over the years in Britain, where the storied racers were built.

DE TOMASO
MANGUSTA 1969

The Mangusta was the second sports-car project brokered by Argentinian Alejandro deTomaso after he gave up racing and moved to Italy with dreams of becoming a manufacturer. His first car, the small, Lotus-like Vallelunga roadster of 1964, attracted little attention. Not so the Mangusta. Low, wide, and menacing on a 98.4-inch wheelbase, it used a strong "backbone" steel chassis, with box-section and tubular members for carrying the powertrain, double-wishbone coil-spring suspension, and beefy all-disc brakes. The Ghia-built body nestled around very broad tires, which were wisely wider at the rear to suit a tail-heavy weight distribution. Dramatic gullwing sections behind the cramped two-seat cockpit provided race-car-like access to the midships Ford V8 and five-speed ZF manual transaxle. Though several hundred pounds heavier than a small-block Cobra, DeTomaso's mongoose had similar power potential and far better aerodynamics. Top speed was a claimed 155 mph, yet price was around $11,500, thousands less than a Ferrari or Lamborghini with comparable performance. Though the basic design was quite impractical for a road car, the Mangusta attracted enough orders to launch DeTomaso as a serious new sports-car marque. It also attracted the attention of America's Rowan Controls company, which soon bought DeTomaso and Ghia as well, thus assuring the future of both.

Having received a bigger small-block V8 for '69, Chevrolet's Corvette entered the Seventies with a bigger big-block, punched out from 427 to 454 cubic inches. Two versions were listed, but only the 390-horsepower four-barrel LS5 unit saw genuine production. *Car and Driver* tested one 'Vette with an LS7 option featuring higher-compression aluminum cylinder heads, high-lift cams, and mechanical lifters, good for 460-465 bhp. Though the magazine reported a sizzling quarter-mile of 13.8 seconds at 108 mph, the LS7 was not readily available, and few if any other '70 Corvettes were so equipped. One reason had to do with an auto workers' strike that delayed initial Corvette sales to February 1970 and nearly halved model-year production to 17,316 units, the lowest total since 1962. Convertibles like this accounted for 6608 units, reflecting the accelerating drop in demand for droptop models through the American industry. Base prices that season were up $4849 for the convertible and $5192 for the T-top coupe.

CHEVROLET
CORVETTE ROADSTER LS5 1970

JAGUAR
SERIES III E-TYPE V-12 1971

It may have resembled earlier E-Types at first glance, but the much-modified Series III of 1971 boasted V12 power, an artifact of Jaguar's super-secret "XJ13" racing-car project of the early Sixties. Replacing the venerable XK six cylinder, the V12 delivered 250 SAE net horsepower from 5.3 liters through four-speed manual or three-speed automatic transmissions. To accommodate the longer engine, the E-Type convertible was reengineered on the same extended chassis as the 2+2 coupe, though the open model was still basically a two-seater. All Series IIIs got a cross-hatch grille insert, reshaped tail, detail updates inside, wider wheels, and reinforcements to the unitized central structure and tubular front subframe. Though heavier than previous E-Types, the V12 would do 0-60 mph in around 7 seconds and well over 130 mph–real Ferrari/Lamborghini stuff. Yet it was far more affordable than the Italians at around $7000 to start in the U.S. This Jaguar lasted into 1975, when production stopped at 15,287, about a fifth of all E-Types ever built.

The Lamborghini Miura had been improving in stages since its 1966 debut. The last and fastest iteration of the iconic mid-V12 coupe was the P400SV, appearing in 1971. Against the previous Miura S, it packed 15 extra horsepower–385 total–thanks to more changes in cam timing and carburetors, plus bigger valves. Other alterations included a larger fuel tank, more effective engine oiling, vented brake rotors (versus solid), and revised rear suspension geometry that raised ride height slightly but improved handling in concert with another upsizing of wheels and tires. The cockpit wasn't ignored either, as switchgear, instruments, and trim were either upgraded, remodeled, or both. The wild Marcello Gandini styling still looked great even after six years and wisely wasn't changed much. However, the SV did get visibly wider rear flanks (to accommodate the broader tires), a discreet ID badge on the tail, and layback headlamps without the surrounding "eyelash" trim that had caused a few giggles on earlier Miuras. With top speed up to 175 mph and acceleration to match, the SV was faster than a Ferrari Daytona and most any other street-legal machine. But Lamborghini was readying an even more outrageous supercar, so the Miura said goodbye in January 1973 when the last SV was sold. Ironically, an unprecedented world energy crisis hit just nine months later, that, at the time, seemed to spell the end for all high-power "exoticars." Fortunately, that pessimistic view would prove to be quite inaccurate.

LAMBORGHINI
MIURA SV 1972

MASERATI
BORA 1973

Maserati swelled the ranks of midengine production sports cars with the 1971 Bora. One of the first projects for designer Giorgetto Giugiaro's new Ital Design studio, the unibody two-seat fastback arrived with a 4.7-liter version of Maserati's familiar racing-derived twincam V8, which sent 310 horsepower to the rear wheels via a manual five-speed transaxle. Striding a 102.2-inch wheelbase, the Bora used classic double-wishbone suspension and rack-and-pinion steering, but also disc brakes with high-pressure hydraulics by Citroën of France, which had recently taken over Maserati and furnished the needed funds for the new model. The hydraulics were also used for power-adjustable pedals, which combined with a tilt/telescope steering wheel for an unusually accommodating Italian cockpit. Tightening emissions limits delayed U.S. sales until 1974, when a substitute 320-bhp 4.9-liter engine solved the problem. Though capable of 160 mph and 0-60 in just 6.5 seconds, the Bora was a civilized supercar, but predictably pricey and rare. Just 571 were built through 1980. Interim changes were few.

Built for Group 4 GT racing and reviving an historic Porsche name, the 1973 Carrera RS boasted a new 230-bhp 2.7-liter flat six, beefed-up chassis, and lightweight coupe bodywork with broader fender flares, bold bodyside graphics, and distinctive "ducktail" rear spoiler. Porsche ran off 1636 RS 2.7s, mainly for Europe, where the model was street legal. A few came to America, but a "dirty" engine meant owners couldn't drive them except on a racetrack.

PORSCHE
911 CARRERA RS 1973

Ferrari finally answered the Lamborghini Miura in 1974 with its own midengine supercar, the 365 GT4 BB. The initials stood for Berlinetta Boxer and signaled a new 4.4-liter horizontally opposed 12-cylinder engine with twin overhead camshafts on each cylinder bank and a rousing 344 DIN horsepower. Such engines are called "boxer" because their pistons pump side to side like the arms of two people sparring. Bodywork, again by Pininfarina, melded steel main panels with aluminum doors, engine lid, and nose cover. Underneath was a complex chassis framework of rectangular and square tubing, plus the expected all-around coil-spring/double-wishbone suspension and four-wheel disc brakes. Though rather heavy at 3420 pounds, the BB decisively raised the bar for high performance, as expected of the successor to the fabled front-V12 Daytona. *Road & Track* ran its BB to 175 mph all out, "the fastest road car we've ever tested." Acceleration was equally vivid, with 0-60 mph in 7.2 seconds, the standing quarter-mile in 15.5 at 102.5 mph. Ferrari built around 400 BBs, then upped the ante in 1976 with the 512 BB. With an enlarged 5.0-liter engine and some 360 bhp, *R&T's* test car clocked 0-60 in just 5.5 seconds and was estimated to reach no less than 188 mph. Modest styling changes carried on for the fuel-injected 512 BBi of 1981, but it claimed "only" 340 bhp due to stricter emissions tuning. Amazingly, these fleet *cavallinos* would soon be overshadowed by even faster Ferraris.

LAMBORGHINI
LP400 COUNTACH 1975

Unveiled as a concept in 1971, the midengine Lamborghini Countach was no less astonishing when sales began in '74. Replacing the Miura, the new LP400 transferred the familiar 5.0-liter twincam V12 to a waist-high Bertone-designed coupe with "scissor" doors and 98.4-inch wheelbase. It was cramped, stiff-riding, and tough to see out of, but who cared? The Countach was Batmobile cool and bat-outta-hell quick, capable of 175 mph and 0-60 in well under 7 seconds. In 1978 came the LP400S with flared fenders, ultrawide wheels and tires, front spoiler, and refinements to suspension and cockpit. It wasn't any faster, but it was somewhat easier to drive in traffic—if you had to. Alas, few Americans got the chance, and then mainly through "gray market" channels, as Lamborghini's mounting financial troubles prevented it from meeting all U.S. standards, thus largely precluding factory sales. That only made the Countach even more the dream ride for "bad boys" with connections and over $50,000 to burn.

BMW
M1 1980

Unveiled in late 1978, the M1 was BMW's first midengine production car, though it was conceived at least five years before as a Porsche 911-beater in production-class racing. BMW lacked experience with "middies," so it contracted chassis development to Lamborghini and body design to Giorgetto Giugiaro's Ital Design. The result was a handsome, if not beautiful, two-seat coupe with a fiberglass skin and a complex multitube chassis. BMW developed a special version of its trademark inline six-cylinder engine, a 3.5 liter with dual overhead cams, four valves per cylinder, and a strong 277 DIN horsepower, delivered through a manual five-speed transaxle. Suspension was naturally all-independent. Wheels were uncommonly large 16-inchers wearing suitably wide, grippy tires. A few 470-bhp racing M1s were built for Europe's 1979-80 "Procar" support series, and a handful of 3.2-liter turbocharged racers had no less than 850 bhp. But BMW had lost interest, so the M1 was discontinued in 1981 after total production of 450 units. Today it's a highly sought-after collector car—and one of the quickest, able to do 0-60 mph in 5.5 seconds and at least 160 mph all out.

In 1984, Enzo Ferrari revived a hallowed old name for his new road/racing car: GTO. Pininfarina's styling themes were familiar and the car used Ferrari's production steel-tube chassis, but its structure was a new mix of fiberglass, aluminum honeycomb, and carbon, Kevlar, and Nomex composites. It was officially the 288 Gran Turismo Omologato. "288" denoted the 2.8-liter twin-turbo V8, which made 395 horsepower at 7000 rpm in road trim, some 600 bhp in racing form. "GTO" made it a GT homologated, or approved, for track competition. As such, it required a cabin suited for two, plus street-legal instrumentation, lights, ground clearance, mirrors, and windshield wipers. Handling was its forte, though even in road spec, it did 0-60 in 5.0 seconds, the quarter-mile in 13.1 at 112 mph. Unfortunately, the international racing series for which it was designed, Group B, dissolved before the GTO had a chance to compete. It cost $83,400, and 200 were built through '87.

FERRARI
288 GTO 1985

A trickle of federalized DeTomaso Panteras made it to the U.S. in the Eighties. Outrageously bespoilered and flared, their image was of a poor-man's Countach. The GT5 of 1980 started it by sticking wheel arches, gapping air dam, and big rear wing onto Pantera's clean original body. Its 1985 successor, the GT5-S, pictured here, integrated those elements for a marginally less tacked-on look. It had a 350-horsepower 5.7-liter Ford V8 and did 5.4 seconds 0-60 mph, 13.6 at 105 in the quarter-mile.

Cooling Testarossa's big flat-12 was critical, and a pair of radiators was located ahead of the rear wheels instead of in the nose. This helped eliminate the circulation of liquids that could overheat the cabin. The size and shape of the inlets also influenced aerodynamics, and Pininfarina had to fit them with horizontal ribs to meet European intake-size limits. The strakes became a copied styling cue. Testarossa weighed 3660 pounds distributed 40/60. It did 0-60 mph in 5.3 seconds, the quarter mile in 13.6 at 105, and reached 178 mph. It got 12 mpg. Its suspension was communicative and surprisingly compliant, its steering informed with slight kickback–a Ferrari characteristic. It was an Eighties icon not revised until 1992, as the 512TR. That version had 421 bhp and a top speed of 187 mph, plus a stiffer chassis and larger, wider tires. A 1994 facelift eliminated the retractable headlamps and brought 440 bhp. But Ferrari called that iteration the 512M, relegating its red head once again to the pages of history.

FERRARI
TESTAROSSA 1987

The name commemorated Ferrari's 40th year as an automaker and was the last Ferrari built while Enzo Ferrari was alive. It took the great man back to his automotive roots. This was no grand touring machine, but a sports car shorn of amenities and packed with power. The chassis used carbon fiber and Kevlar, and the lightweight plastic body was shaped to provide aerodynamic downforce at the car's 196-mph top speed. Fuel was stored in two rubber-celled tanks, and fire-resistant Nomex served as the upholstery. Pull cords opened the doors, and there was no carpeting. Antilock brakes were not offered, the F40 relying instead on huge discs and the driver's ability. Lifting the louvered tail section revealed a 2.9-liter twincam V8 with dual turbos and 478 horsepower, enough to shoot the 3018-pound car from 0-60 mph in 3.8 seconds. A conventional five-speed manual was the transmission. The F40 cost $470,000, and each of the 1000 built was a collector piece. It was unveiled in July 1987. Enzo Ferrari died on August 14, 1988.

FERRARI
F40 1988

The Porsche 959 was a towering technological achievement that combined levels of acceleration, top speed, and all-around control rivaled by precious few automobiles in history. Built as a racing car, its Group B competition series disbanded before it could run, and the world was left with a roadgoing sports car of fabled reputation. Porsche's engineering obsession was unreined for this one and though the car looked something like the 911 coupe on which its was based, the 959 was far different in function and design. It had all-wheel drive, unholy power, and a body ducted, spoilered, and widened to suit its stratospheric needs. Production was limited to just 230 during the mid-Eighties. A competition version, the 961, proved itself by winning the punishing Paris-Dakar Rally in 1984 and '86. Production versions were offered in 1987 and '88 in "Comfort" and lighter "Sport" form. The 959 was too specialized to be sold in the U.S., and though a handful came stateside, most stayed in Europe where transaction prices routinely topped the $230,000 retail price. The ultimate Porsche to many, it was, in the words of renowned racer and writer Paul Frere, "a new dimension in motoring."

PORSCHE
959 1988

Flanking the 959's steel central body were functional aerodynamic panels of lightweight Kevlar and other advanced materials. The engine was a flat-six but used water-cooled heads, two turbochargers, and other advanced features to get 450 horsepower from just 2.8 liters. A six-speed manual was the sole transmission. Weight was 3088 pounds, top speed 190 mph, and 0-60 mph came in just 3.7 seconds. A multiplate clutch acted as a front differential, and torque apportioning was computer-governed or followed one of four driver-selected programs, from locked front and rear to 20/80 in full acceleration. Suspension departed from the 911 with double wishbones and computer-controlled coil-over shocks with soft, firm, and automatic damping modes, plus three ride heights. Some of these elements made their way into subsequent Porsches, but the 959 stands apart as a signal achievement.

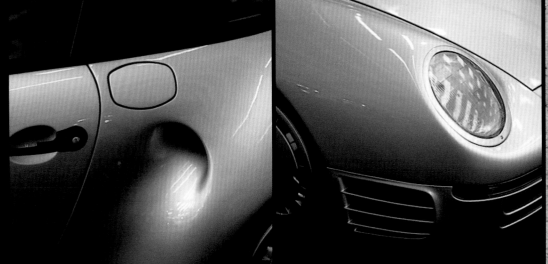

Lamborghini marked its 25th year as an automaker in 1988 with the Anniversary Edition Countach. The 5.2 V12 was unchanged, but the body got rocker-panel strakes and air intakes that were more gracefully integrated with the rear fenders. Composite plastics replaced aluminum for these and other exterior components. Some of this was the influence of Chrysler Corporation, which had purchased Lamborghini in 1987 for $30 million. Its intent was a more livable supercar, and, to that end, the Anniversary Edition also benefitted from more comfortable seats and added sound insulation. None of this detracted from performance, which the factory listed as 4.7 seconds 0-60, 12.9 in the quarter-mile, and a top speed of 183. This was the final Countach, and critics said it was the best since the original if not the finest of all. For certain, it was the best-selling Countach ever, with 650 built through the end of production in 1990.

LAMBORGHINI
COUNTACH 1989

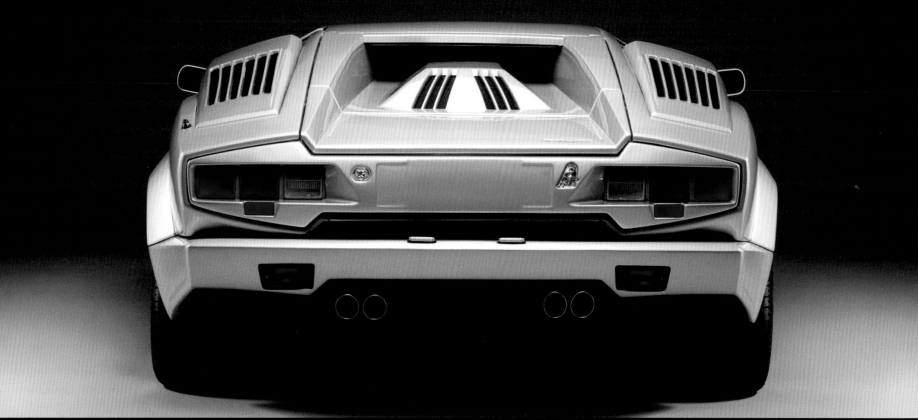

Rumors about it had circulated for years, and by late 1989 it was ready: the ZR1. Actually a $27,000 option for the $32,000 1990 Corvette coupe, the ZR1 extended the Corvette credo of world-class performance at middle-class prices to a new level. Fans called it King of the Hill, and some paid $100,000 for the first examples off the assembly line—then put them in storage. The ZR1's Ferrari-like performance helped give GM a needed image boost, though its only visual distinction from other 'Vettes was squared-off taillamps set into a wider, convex tail, a design needed to accommodate its wider rear tires. The FX3 adjustable suspension with touring, sport, and performance settings was standard. The ZR1 arrived with a revamped interior that introduced a driver-side airbag, a design common to all '90 Corvettes. A showcase of powertrain technology, the ZR1 would be offered through 1995, and a total of 6939 were produced.

CHEVROLET
CORVETTE ZR1 1990

After considering a variety of homegrown turbo powerplants, Chevy got Britain's Lotus to design a sophisticated naturally aspirated V8. Dubbed the LT5 and built by Mercury Marine in Oklahoma, the all-alloy dohc 32-valve 5.7 had 375 horsepower and came with a console-mounted "valet key" that cut power to about 210 bhp. It propelled the 3500-pound coupe from 0-60 mph in 4.5 seconds, through the quarter-mile in 12.4 at 111 mph, and to a top speed of 175. Plus it averaged 17 mpg city/26 highway. A six-speed manual was the only available transmission. Horsepower would rise to 405 for 1993. ZR1 showed America could produce world-class performance and helped propel the sports car into a new golden age.

True to tradition, Lamborghini's supercar for the nineties was named for a fighting bull, but Diablo is another word for devil. Indeed, it certainly had enough power to feel possessed. Lamborghini engineers succeeded in the formidable task of creating a new car that one-upped the Countach while retaining its heritage and meeting modern-day safety and emissions standards. The Diablo was the only Lamborghini developed under Chrysler, which furnished computer-design expertise and also softened the lines of designer Marcello Gandini's original styling. The 492-bhp, 5.7-liter V12's performance was appropriately ferocious, with 4.5-second 0-60 times and a 202-mph top speed.

By 1996, the Diablo line had expanded to include the all-wheel-drive VT roadster, the lightweight SV with flashy body side graphics, and the race-ready SVR.

VECTOR
W-8 1991

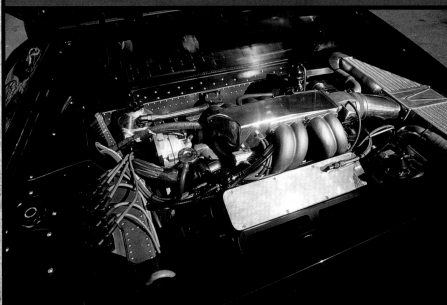

Operating on the fringes of credibility was Vector Aeromotive Corporation, which raised $20 million in 1988 to build a Ferrari-beating midengine supercar but was suspiciously broke within a few years after producing fewer than 30 automobiles. The W2 Twin Turbo pictured here is typical of the variations on a theme Vector periodically unveiled to keep press and public baited. It purported to use military aircraft technology and had an aluminum honeycomb structure, composite body, and a twin-turbo 5.7-liter V8 of a claimed 600 bhp. Subsequent owners did produce a V12 Vector, but neither car nor company would last.

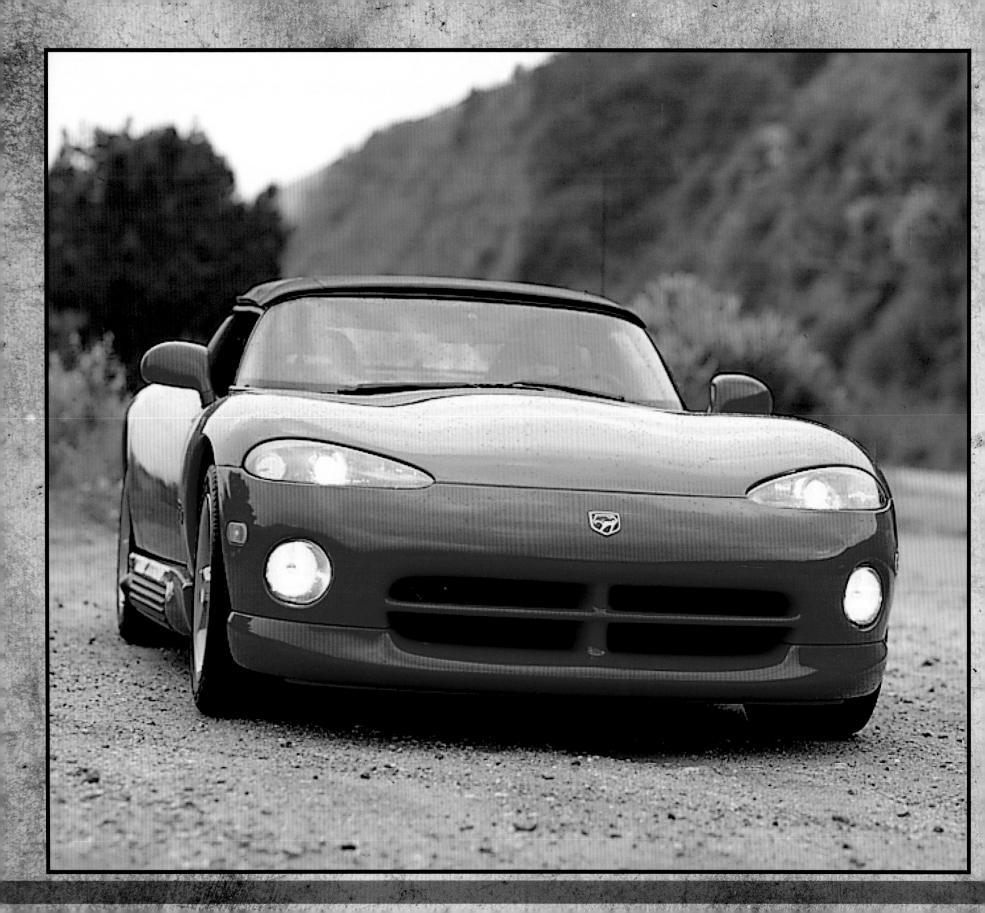

DODGE
VIPER 1992

Chrysler revived the spirit of the hallowed 1960s Shelby Cobra 427SC with the milestone Dodge Viper RT/10. After a show-stopping concept debut at the 1989 Detroit Auto Show and a whirlwind development cycle, production Vipers were ready for the 1992 model year. A true roadster, Viper was an unapologetic celebration of American brute horsepower unencumbered by high-tech gadgetry or creature comforts.

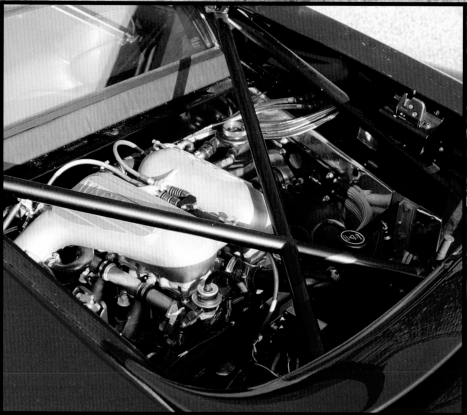

The Jaguar XJ220 drew much praise—and collected more than 1000 order deposits—when it was first shown in 1988 as a concept vehicle. That original XJ220 concept boasted a V12 engine and projected top speed of 220 mph, but much had changed by the time the car went on sale in 1992 as a production model. The V12 was replaced by a 540-horsepower 3.5-liter V6 version of the engine that powered Jaguar racecars, and all-wheel drive was replaced by rear-wheel drive. A production XJ220 was timed at 217.1 mph—not quite 220, but fast enough to take the Guinness World Record as the fastest standard production car. The 0-60 mph time was a blistering 3.6 seconds. In spite of the XJ220's high performance, sales were disappointing—only 271 examples were built. Many potential buyers didn't like the substitution of a V6 engine, and an early-Nineties recession significantly hampered the supercar market.

JAGUAR
XJ220 1992

Introduced in Europe in 1994 and the U.S. in 1996, the DB7 was the first Aston Martin developed under Ford Motor Company, which took control of Aston in 1987. Aston Martin wisely revived the DB name, which had been dropped in 1972, for this model. Ford money helped develop, test, and certify the car, but the DB7 was designed by Aston to be an Aston. Available in both coupe and Volante convertible versions, the voluptuous body was styled by Aston's Ian Callum, formerly of Ford's Ghia studio, with subtle nods to DBs of the past. A refined dohc inline-six put out 335 bhp with the help of an Eaton supercharger and propelled the DB7 to 5.5-second 0-60 times and a 165-mph top speed when equipped with the standard five-speed manual transmission.

ASTON MARTIN
DB7 1994

Sumptuous interiors featured Connolly hide upholstery, deep-pile carpet, and burr walnut dashboard and console trim. Production of under 700 cars per year guaranteed exclusivity, as did the $125,000 sticker price. A top-line DB7 Vantage was introduced for 1999. Its 6.0-liter V12 put out 420 bhp and was good for top speeds of over 180 mph. Although underwritten by Ford, these cars represented the summit of British automaking.

Just as the Dodge Viper RT/10 roadster paid tribute to the Shelby Cobra roadster, the Viper GTS coupe was a Nineties paean to the Shelby Cobra Daytona Coupe. The vehicle shown is Dodge's 1995 concept car, but production versions that followed for the 1996 model year were virtually identical in appearance, right down to the "skunk" stripes and competition-look aluminum fuel-filler cap. The coupe body style added a sliver of civility to the Viper's brutish nature, with standard driver- and passenger-side airbags, air-conditioning, power windows, electric door-latches, a security system, adjustable pedals, and a six-disc CD changer. Despite the added features, the GTS coupe was actually 70 pounds lighter than the RT/10 roadster, and faster too. *Road & Track* spurred a 1996 GTS on to a 4.4-second 0-60 sprint and a 12.8-second quarter-mile run.

DODGE
VIPER 1996

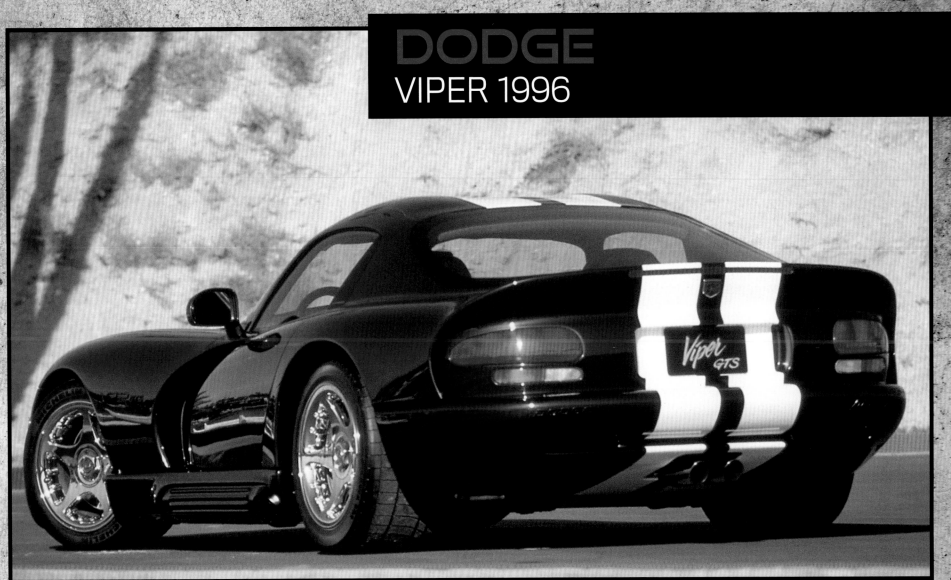

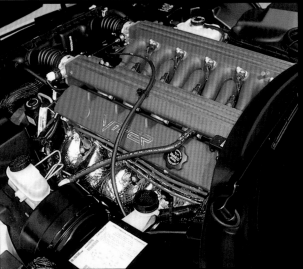

Skidpad and slalom numbers were a tick better than the roadster's as well. Production 1996 GTS engines were rated at 450 bhp, 35 more than their roadster counterparts. A new aluminum engine block, improved heads, a lumpier camshaft, and a less restrictive exhaust were responsible for the gain; roadster models received the same upgrades in 1997. In 1999, an ACR (American Club Racer) package was added for those who wanted to race their Vipers on weekends. The $10,000 package included racing tires and suspension, five-point seat-belt harness, ACR nameplates and graphics, and deleted the air-conditioning, radio, and fog lights. Antilock brakes were not available until the 2001 model year, when Dodge introduced them as a standard feature. First-generation Vipers would reign until the 2003 model year, when they were replaced with a redesigned roadster with even more horsepower. Total 1992–2002 Viper production was over 14,000.

Like Porsche with the 911, Lotus refined and fortified the Esprit over the years. The evergreen Esprit evolved from a naturally aspirated sports car with as little as 140 bhp to a turbocharged one with as much as 300. In 1996 Lotus replaced the turbo four with the line's first V8 engine. The 350-hp twin-turbo 3.5 kept the Esprit's performance solidly into the supercar realm, with 4.5-second 0-60 times and a top speed of 178 mph. The Esprit's radical "door-stop" styling, aided by a 1987 freshening, still turned heads, but by the mid-nineties the overall design was showing its 20-year-old roots. Trundling along in traffic could be a real chore, due to the Esprit's noisy, claustrophobic cockpit, near-zero rear visibility, and weak torque below 3000 rpm. But out on a twisty, uncluttered road, screaming up near its 6900 rpm redline, it delivered joyous performance. High-speed handling was exemplary, with body-roll-free cornering and stable braking. Part of the Esprit's appeal was sheer rarity; its yearly production was always miniscule. Only 260 1996 models were built.

LOTUS
ESPRIT 1996

MCLAREN
F1 1996

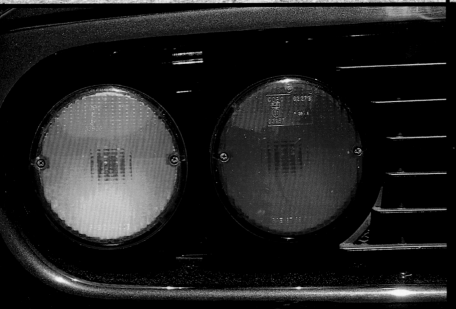

Drawing on multiple Formula 1, CanAm, and Indianapolis victories, England's McLaren organization set about creating its first road car in 1989. Revealed to the public in 1992, the McLaren F1 was on the road by 1994 and in the winner's circle at LeMans in 1995. With its no-holds-barred engineering, the F1 redefined the term "supercar." Scissor-type doors provided access to a leather interior with an unusual "1+2" layout: a form-fitting driver seat was centrally located, with a passenger seat slightly aft on both sides. A BMW-designed 6.1-liter V12 was mounted amidships and packed 627 bhp. A carbon-fiber body/chassis structure made for an unprecedented power-to-weight ratio of under four lbs per horsepower. Price and performance were equally stratospheric: $810,000, 0-60 in 3.2 seconds, 11.1-second quarter-mile times, and a 231-mph top speed. Ninety-five mph was possible in second gear. When production ceased in 1997, only 100 cars, including GTR and LeMans competition versions, had been built.

PANOZ
ESPERANTE 2000

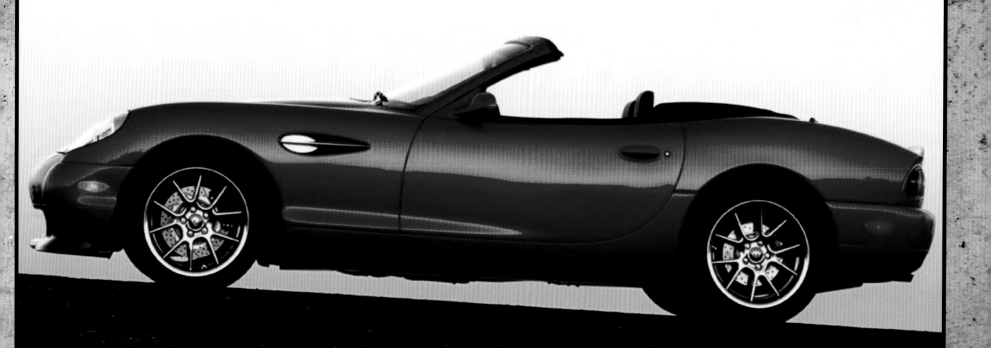

The product of one of America's smallest viable auto manufacturers, the Panoz Esperante boasted a Ford powertrain and an all-aluminum chassis. A version of the same engine found in some Mustangs, the 4.6-liter V8 produced 320 bhp. Esperantes were expensive and rare. Introduced in 2000 with an $80,000 price tag, fewer than 200 were produced annually. Under hood stainless-steel plates bore the signatures of the craftsmen who hand assembled each car.

Replacing the short-lived hardtop in the Corvette lineup, the Z06 became the ultimate expression of Chevrolet's long-lived sports car. Introduced in 2001, the Z06 featured the firmest suspension in the 'Vette stable and a breathed-on version of the standard 5.7-liter V8, good for 385 horsepower. Power jumped to 405 bhp for 2002. The bargain of the supercar crowd, the $53,000 Z06 was clocked reaching 60 mph in 4.5 seconds by *Road & Track*, on par with Ferrari's $170,000 Modena. Visible here are the red calipers of the Z06's enhanced brakes. With an all-new "C6" Corvette due for 2005, Chevrolet dropped the Z06 after 2004, planning to replace it with an even higher-performance version by 2006.

CHEVROLET
CORVETTE Z06 2001

LAMBORGHINI
MURCIELAGO 2002

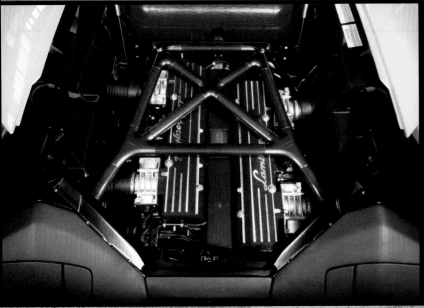

Next in line to carry the Lamborghini's supercar torch, Murciélago took over where the Diablo left off. New for 2002, a roadster joined the line in 2004. Though Murciélago means "bat" in Spanish, the stealthy implications of the name were lost on these cars. The beefy Lambo V12 returned for Murciélago duty, enlarged to 6.2 liters, up from the Diablo's 6.0. Producing a prodigious 575 bhp, the Italian sports car reached 60 mph in a scant 3.7 seconds, according to *Motor Trend*. Top speed was in excess of 200 mph. Rare among exotics, Murciélago put power to the ground through a full-time all-wheel-drive system. Murciélago prices started at $280,000.

Redone for 2003, Dodge's brutal Viper got a new body and an additional helping of power. Viper's 8.0-liter V10 grew to 8.3 liters, adding 50 bhp for an even 500. Performance was startling, with a 0-60 time of 4.1 seconds and a top speed approaching 180 mph. A single SRT-10 convertible model replaced the previous generation's RT/10 droptop and GTS coupe. Refinements for 2003 included a 100-pound weight reduction, a 2.3-inch longer wheelbase, and a return to the signature side exhaust outlets that disappeared in 1996. A six-speed manual was the standard and only transmission available. Base price in 2003: $79,995.

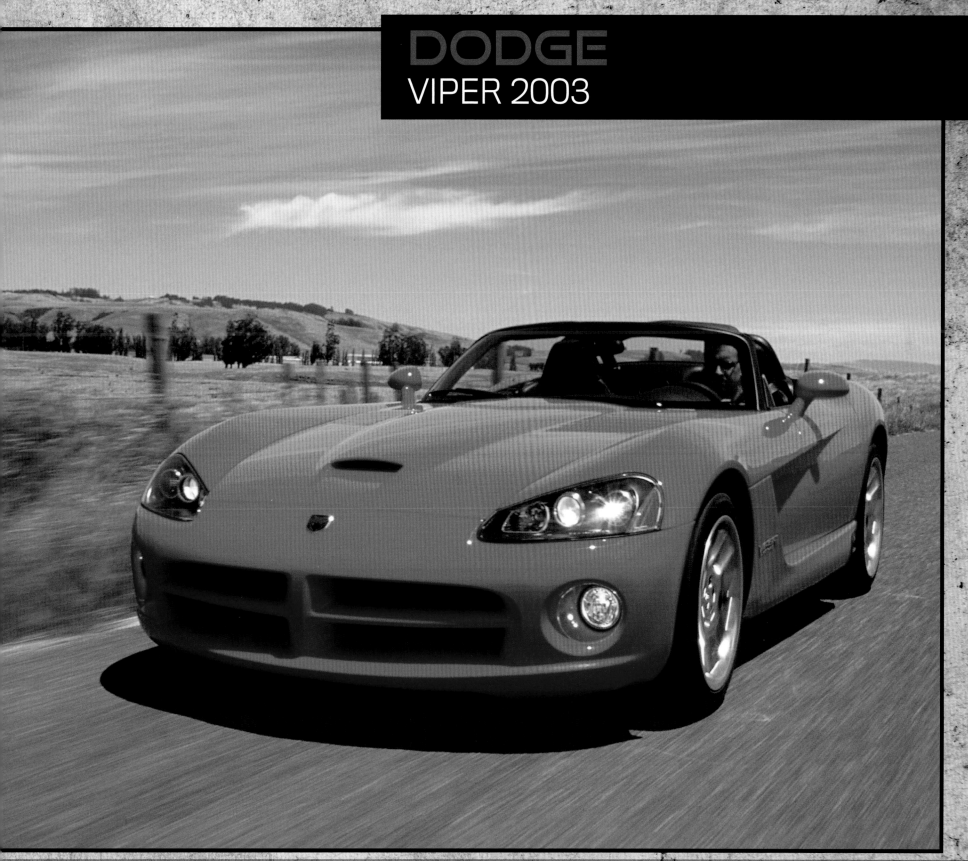

DODGE
VIPER 2003

The crown jewel of the Ferrari lineup, the limited-production Enzo came and went in the blink of an eye. Applying the company's famous "demand minus one" formula, Ferrari built just 399 of the stunning coupes–all in 2003 and 2004. Extracting 660 horsepower from a 6.0-liter midship-mounted V12, and weighing less than 3000 pounds, performance was eye-popping. According to *Road & Track* magazine, the Enzo sprang from 0-60 mph in a scant 3.3 seconds, and topped out at nearly 220 mph. Equally breathtaking was the Enzo's price, about $650,000. The only available transmission was a 6-speed clutchless "sequential" manual unit with steering-wheel-mounted paddle shifters. Extensive use of exotic materials helped make Ferrari's lithe dancer the welterweight it was. Body panels were formed of a carbon fiber and Nomex "sandwich," while the chassis and tub were formed of carbon fiber. Named for the company's founder who died in August 1988, the car's official name was Ferrari Enzo Ferrari, but fans and the press quickly reduced it to simply Enzo. Color choices were limited to yellow, black, and Ferrari's trademark red. Guaranteeing the Enzo's rarity stateside, Ferrari shipped only 100 cars to America.

FERRARI
ENZO 2003

SALEEN
S7 2003

Best known for its aggressively modified Mustangs, Saleen Engineering entered the production sports car business in 2003 with the wildly extroverted S7. A true American supercar, the S7 boasted a massive 7.0-liter Ford-based V8 and a trim 2800 pound curb weight. Performance was predictably stunning–*Car and Driver* drove an S7 to 60 mph in 3.3 seconds. Price: $395,000.

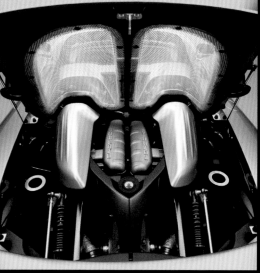

Bearing a name synonymous with sports cars, Porsche was not about to be left out of the supercar renaissance. The stunning Carrera GT arrived on the scene for 2004, and moved promptly to the head of the Porsche class. The GT boasted Porsche's largest-ever street-going engine, a 5.7-liter V10. With 605 bhp on tap, the midship-mounted-engine moved the 3000-pound GT to 60 mph in a factory-claimed 3.9 seconds. Top speed was reported to be in excess of 200 mph. To make the most of the car's limited storage space, Porsche included a matching five-piece luggage set with each car. Price: just under $400,000.

BUGATTI
VEYRON 2005

Bugatti's twenty-first-century renaissance began with Veyron and its promised 1001-horsepower V16. Federalized models actually delivered 987 horsepower, roughly double Viper's power output. Production began for 2005, and was limited to 50 vehicles annually. Now under Volkswagen control, the latest Bugatti revival was free of the financial limitations that killed a 1990's rebirth effort.

Although planned as GT40, a breakdown in negotiations prevented Ford from licensing use of the GT40 moniker for its 2005 reinvention of the legendary LeMans racer. By production time, the all-new supercar was known simply as GT. Recalling its 1966 LeMans victory over Ferrari, Ford again set its sights on outperforming the Italian sports car builder, this time aiming to outgun its 360 Maranello. Power targets were impressive, 500 bhp and 500 pound-feet of torque from the GT's supercharged-5.4-liter V8. Intended to be a technological *tour de force*, the GT's credentials were impressive. Ultrastiff floor panels were formed of a lightweight mesh graphite and aluminum "sandwich." The rigid space frame and body panels were aluminum.

FORD
GT 2005

Recalling the glory of Mercedes' 1950s racing success, the 2005 SLR McLaren probed the limits of front-engine performance. With a body and chassis codeveloped with McLaren Racing Development, and a heavily massaged version of Mercedes' already impressive supercharged V8, the SLR was granted instant supercar status. Weighing in at approximately 3000 pounds, and with more than 600 bhp on tap, performance was breathtaking. The SLR's flip-open doors recalled the "gullwing" arrangement of early SL coupes. High-tech features included a carbon-fiber chassis and ceramic brakes. Price: around $350,000.

MERCEDES-BENZ
SLR MCLAREN 2005

CHEVROLET
CORVETTE Z06 2015

The C7-generation Chevrolet Corvette that arrived in 2014 was significantly lighter and stiffer than the C6 Corvette it replaced. A new "King of the Hill" version came one year later with the revival of the super-performance Z06 model. The C7 Z06 had a supercharged 6.2-liter V8 with 650 horsepower and 650 pound-feet of torque, which enabled it to accelerate from 0-60 mph in 3.2 seconds with the 7-speed manual transmission, or a jaw-dropping 2.95 seconds with the 8-speed automatic. *Road & Track* achieved a top speed of 186 mph. In spite of its incredible performance, the Z06 was surprisingly livable in everyday driving. Plus, the base price began at under $80,000–a fraction of the cost of other supercars with comparable capabilities.

LAMBORGHINI
AVENTADOR S 2016

Ferruccio Lamborghini chose a charging bull as the emblem for his car company, and had a tradition of naming models after famous fighting bulls. That practice continued under the Lamborghini firm's various corporate owners over the years—the Aventador, which debuted as a 2011 model, was named for a fighting bull from the Nineties. For 2016, an Aventador S version was introduced; it featured a more sophisticated suspension and a four-wheel steering system that allowed sharper steering at low speeds and better stability at high speeds. There was also a more powerful 740-horsepower 6.5-liter V12 that could push the all-wheel- drive, mid-engine supercar to 217 mph, with 0-62 mph coming in just 2.9 seconds. The S's base price was around $450,000.

Acura first dipped a toe into the mid-engine exotic-car market for 1991, when it introduced the NSX—a two-seat, mid-engine supercar powered by a naturally aspirated V6. The first-generation NSX was a pragmatic exotic, offering outstanding reliability and ergonomics, but perhaps not inspiring the same level of irrational passion as its European rivals. Production of the first NSX lasted from 1991 to 2005, and no major changes were made over the model's lifespan. After a long gestation period, a reborn NSX finally debuted for 2017. The second-generation model was an all-wheel- drive hybrid with a twin-turbo 3.5-liter V6 and three electric motors. One motor was integrated with a 9-speed dual-clutch automatic transmission and joined the gas engine in powering the rear wheels; the other two motors drove the front wheels. The combined output of all motors was 573 horsepower. According to *Road & Track*, the rakish hybrid was capable of accelerating 0-60 mph in 3.1 seconds and had an estimated top speed of 191 mph. The NSX was an exotic that was refined, reliable, and had the added bonus of respectable fuel economy from its state-of- the-art hybrid drivetrain.

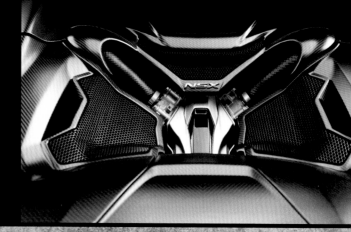

ACURA
NSX 2017

BUGATTI
CHIRON 2017

There are supercars, and then there are supercars, and the Bugatti Chiron definitely qualifies as the latter. The Chiron's quad-turbocharged 8.0-liter W-16 engine developed an astonishing 1500 horsepower and 1180 pound-feet of torque—enough for a 0-60 mph time of 2.4 seconds and an electronically limited top speed of 261 mph. A Haldex all-wheel- drive system got all that power to the road with the least amount of drama. The Chiron set a world record by accelerating 0 to 400 km/h (248 mph) and then braking to a stop in 41.96 seconds. That record was quickly bettered by Koenigsegg, but it was still a remarkable accomplishment. Base price for the Chiron was around $3,000,000. As expected at that price, there was no visible plastic in the cockpit—only top-grade leather and metal. The Chiron was more refined and quiet than its predecessor, the Bugatti Veyron, and was also surprisingly docile at low speeds.

FERRARI
LAFERRARI 2017

Ferrari would probably be the last make expected to sell a hybrid, but the LaFerrari was no ordinary hybrid—it combined a 788-horsepower V12 with a 161-hp electric motor for a total 949 hp. Introduced for 2013, the LaFerrari hybrid was even faster than Ferrari's celebrated 2003-04 Enzo model—it could rocket from 0-60 mph in less than three seconds and hit a top speed of 217 mph. Plus, the weight of the low-mounted battery packs lowered the car's center of gravity and improved handling. The LaFerrari's price tag was a cool $1.4 million, but Ferrari had no trouble selling 500 coupes, as well as 210 Aperta convertible versions. The final LaFerrari Aperta was sold at an auction in 2017 for $9.96 million, with proceeds supporting the Save the Children charity.

FORD
GT 2017

To celebrate the 50th anniversary of the Ford GT40's historic 1966 Le Mans victory, Ford designed an all-new GT racecar for the 2016 24 Hours of Le Mans. The new GTs did their legendary forebears proud, finishing first, third, fourth, and ninth in the GTE Pro Class. The production GT was closely related to the racing version, and lacked the luxury features often found on other high-end supercars. The GT's cockpit was a tight fit for two passengers, and cargo room was almost nonexistent. The payoff was reduced weight, with racecar-like performance and handling. The EcoBoost 3.5-liter V6 shared its basic engine block with the Ford F-150, but developed 647 horsepower and was capable of traveling from 0-60 mph in 2.9 seconds and reaching a top speed of 216 mph, according to *Car and Driver*. The price was around $450,000, and Ford planned to build 1000 examples over the 2017–2020 model years.

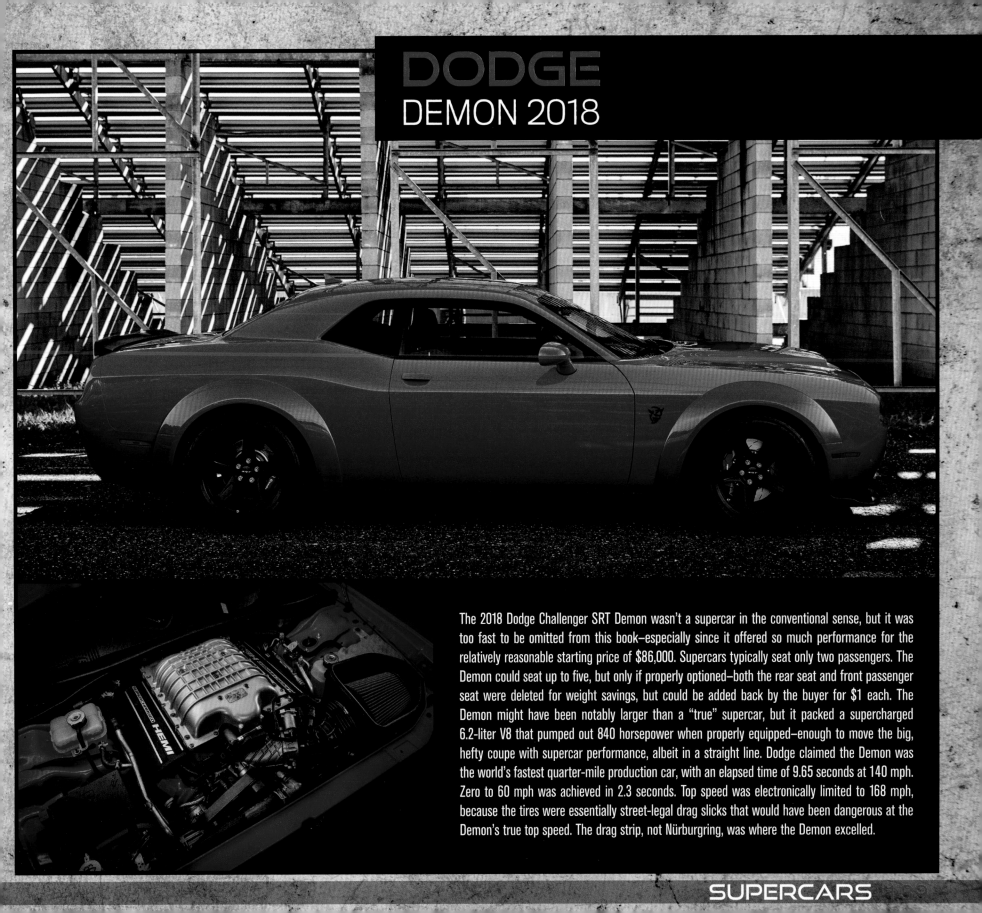

DODGE
DEMON 2018

The 2018 Dodge Challenger SRT Demon wasn't a supercar in the conventional sense, but it was too fast to be omitted from this book—especially since it offered so much performance for the relatively reasonable starting price of $86,000. Supercars typically seat only two passengers. The Demon could seat up to five, but only if properly optioned—both the rear seat and front passenger seat were deleted for weight savings, but could be added back by the buyer for $1 each. The Demon might have been notably larger than a "true" supercar, but it packed a supercharged 6.2-liter V8 that pumped out 840 horsepower when properly equipped—enough to move the big, hefty coupe with supercar performance, albeit in a straight line. Dodge claimed the Demon was the world's fastest quarter-mile production car, with an elapsed time of 9.65 seconds at 140 mph. Zero to 60 mph was achieved in 2.3 seconds. Top speed was electronically limited to 168 mph, because the tires were essentially street-legal drag slicks that would have been dangerous at the Demon's true top speed. The drag strip, not Nürburgring, was where the Demon excelled.

KOENIGSEGG
AGERE RS 2018

Koenigsegg is a small, independent manufacturer based in Sweden that started building cars in the mid-Nineties. At the time of this book's publication, the Koenigsegg Agere RS was the fastest car in world, with an official time of 277.9 mph for a two-way average on an 11-mile stretch of highway in Nevada. Actually, the Agere RS's best time was 284.6 mph, but official testing requires an average of travel in both directions. Previously, Koenigsegg broke a record set by Bugatti by accelerating 0 to 400 km/h (248 mph) and then braking to a stop in 36.44 seconds. The Agere RS was powered by a twin-turbocharged 5.0-liter V8 with 1341 horsepower and 1011 pound feet of torque, and cost in the neighborhood of $2 million.

Although McLaren Automotive had its roots in racing, the McLaren 720S wasn't an uncomfortable, uncompromising performance car. In fact, the 720S was one of the most civilized supercars, boasting a quiet, smooth ride and docile manners in around-town driving. However, that doesn't mean that this English-built, mid-engine supercar lacked speed; its twin-turbo 4.0-liter V8 developed 710 horsepower and was capable of 212 mph. Zero-60 mph took 2.8 seconds, and 0-100 mph came in only 5.5 seconds. Extensive use of carbon fiber helped bring the curb weight down to a reasonable 2828 pounds, and a computer-controlled active suspension provided both a comfortable ride and excellent handling. The 720S's base price was around $285,000.

MCLAREN
720S 2018

SUPERCARS

SPYKER
C8 PRELIATOR 2018

The Netherlands isn't the first country that comes to mind when exotic supercars are discussed, but that's where Spyker Cars is headquartered. The company, which was founded in 1999, revives the name of a Dutch manufacturer that built 4-wheel- drive 6-cylinder cars as early as 1903, and also produced airplanes during World War I. Even among their lavishly appointed supercar rivals, Spyker cars stand out for their meticulously crafted, retro-look cockpits. The Spyker C8 Preliator was a mid-engine exotic that was initially offered with an Audi-sourced 4.2-liter supercharged V8. For 2018, Spyker arranged to buy 600-horsepower 5.0-liter V8s from supercar builder Koenigsegg. With the new powerplant, the C8 Preliator was expected to accelerate from 0-60 mph in 3.6 seconds and achieve a top speed of 201 mph. The Preliator's base price was around $430,000, and a production run of 50 coupes and 100 convertibles was planned.

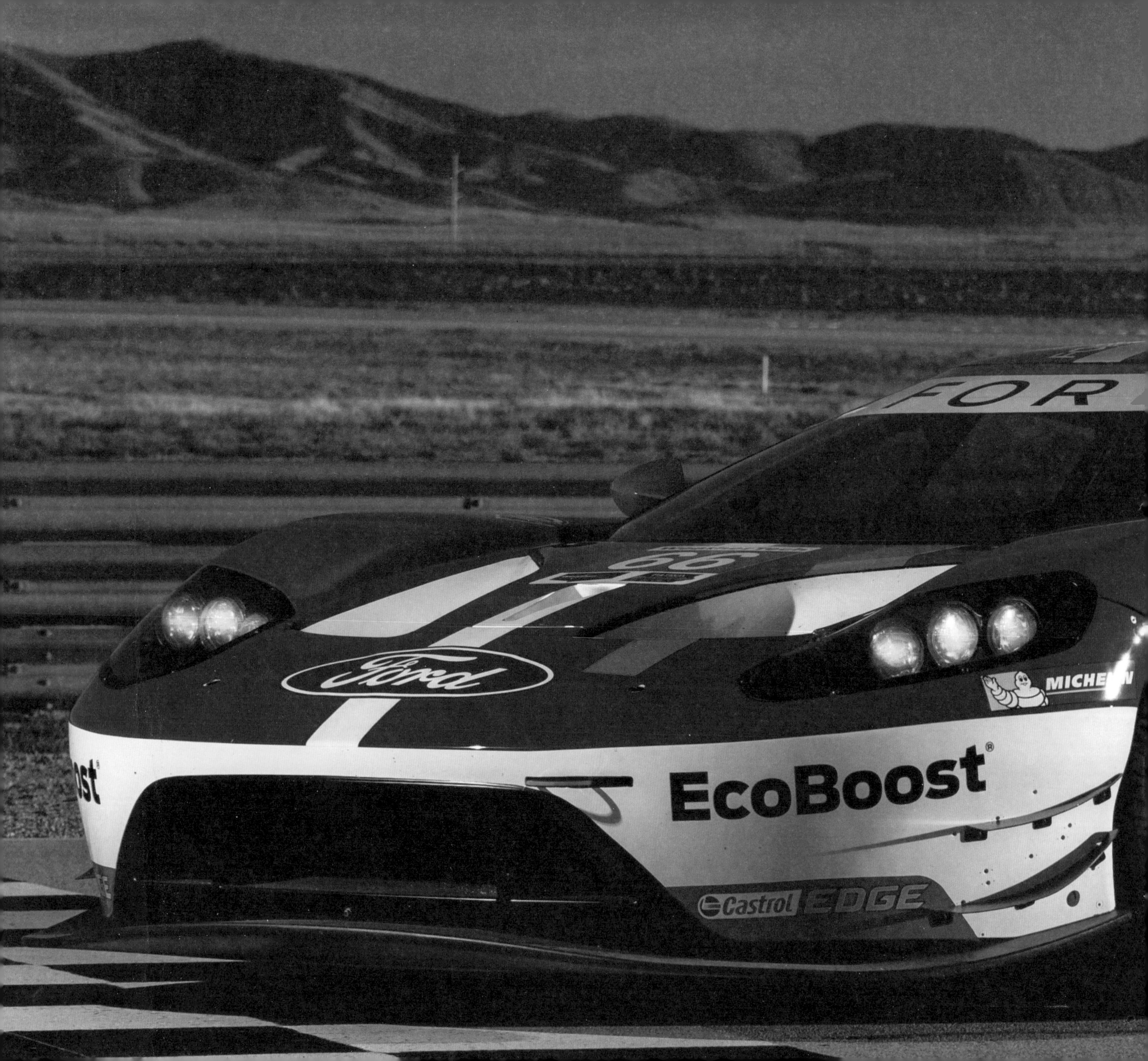

FOR
Ford
MICHELIN
EcoBoost
Castrol EDGE